6/04

First Facts™

Our Physical World

Friction

by Ellen Sturm Niz

Consultant:
Philip W. Hammer, PhD
Vice President, The Franklin Center
The Franklin Institute
Philadelphia, Pennsylvania

Capstone
press
Mankato, Minnesota

First Facts is published by Capstone Press,
151 Good Counsel Drive, P.O. Box 669, Mankato, Minnesota 56002.
www.capstonepress.com

Library of Congress Cataloging-in-Publication Data
Niz, Ellen Sturm.
    Friction / by Ellen Sturm Niz; consultant, Philip W. Hammer.
    p. cm.—(First facts. Our physical world)
    Includes bibliographical references and index.
    ISBN–13: 978-0-7368-5402-3 (hardcover)
    ISBN–10: 0-7368-5402-9 (hardcover)
    1. Friction—Experiments—Juvenile literature. I. Title. II. Series.
QC197.N59 2006
531'.1134'078—dc22   2005013323

Summary: Introduces young readers to friction, its characteristics, and its uses in the world.
    Includes instructions for an activity to demonstrate some of friction's characteristics.

Editorial Credits
Aaron Sautter, editor; Linda Clavel, set designer; Bobbi J. Dey, book designer;
    Scott Thoms, illustrator; Kelly Garvin, photo researcher/photo editor

Photo Credits
Capstone Press/Karon Dubke, cover, 5, 6 (both), 8–9, 10, 11, 14–15, 21
Corbis/TempSport, 18–19
Getty Images Inc./Hulton Archive, 13
Index Stock Imagery/Jim McGuire, 17
Peter Arnold Inc./Astrofoto, 20

Table of Contents

Friction

Have you tried sledding without snow? It isn't much fun. You have to push hard to make the sled move. **Friction** keeps the sled from sliding easily down the hill.

Friction is the force that slows objects down when they rub together. Rough things, like grass, create more friction than smooth things, like snow.

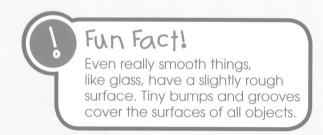

Fun Fact!

Even really smooth things, like glass, have a slightly rough surface. Tiny bumps and grooves cover the surfaces of all objects.

Static and Kinetic Friction

A toy box will not slide by itself. **Static** friction keeps it from moving. Static friction is the force that holds objects in place when they are not moving.

If you push on the toy box, it will slide across the floor. When the box is moving, **kinetic** friction works against, or **resists,** the movement. Kinetic friction is the force that slows down moving objects.

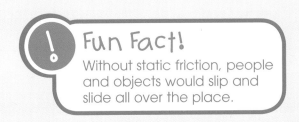

Fun Fact!
Without static friction, people and objects would slip and slide all over the place.

Rolling Friction

Rolling friction occurs when a round object rolls across a surface. It is easier to push a toy car on its wheels than on its side. The car's round wheels touch only a small area. Less friction is created, and the car moves more easily.

Fun Fact!
Rolling friction still slows down moving objects. If you stop pushing on it, the car will slow down and stop.

8

Weight and Friction

The amount of friction between objects depends on how hard objects push against each other. An empty wagon is not very heavy. It's easy to pull.

A wagon full of friends is heavier. The wagon pushes harder against the ground. More friction is created, so it is harder to pull the heavy wagon.

Guillaume Amontons

French scientist Guillaume Amontons was the first to discover that heavy objects create more friction. He did experiments with weight and friction in the 1600s.

Amontons found that heavy objects create more friction by pushing down harder than lighter objects. Today, his discoveries are called Amontons' Laws of Friction.

Amontons (holding telescope) also invented or improved several scientific instruments.

Heat and Friction

Friction between objects always creates heat. Rubbing your hands together can make them warm in cold weather. The friction between your hands creates heat.

Heat from friction can be useful. If a Boy Scout rubs two sticks together fast enough, he can light a campfire.

Reducing Friction

Lubricants help reduce friction. They fill the tiny bumps and grooves on the surfaces of objects. This lets objects slide over each other easily.

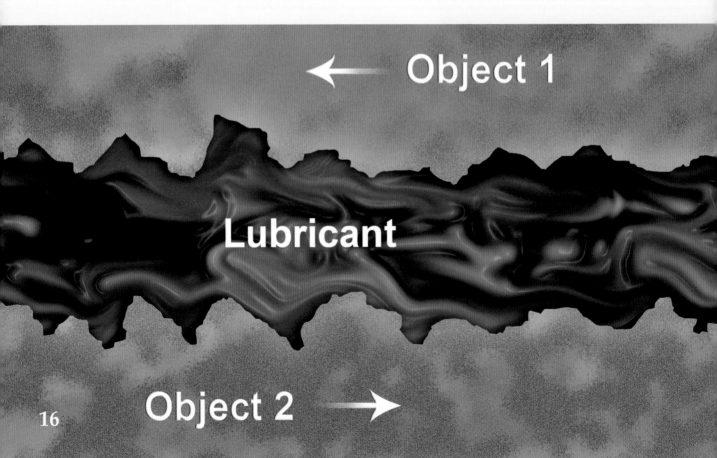

Object 1 ←

Lubricant

Object 2 →

Water acts as a slick lubricant between you and a water slide. Zoom! And you're down the slide! Oil, grease, and wax are other lubricants people use.

Using Friction

Friction has many uses. Gymnasts use chalk on their hands to create friction so they don't slip off the parallel bars. Friction helps a car's tires grip the road. Friction is a force people use every day.

 Fun Fact!
Friction is helping you right now. It helps you hold onto this book. It even keeps you from sliding out of your chair!

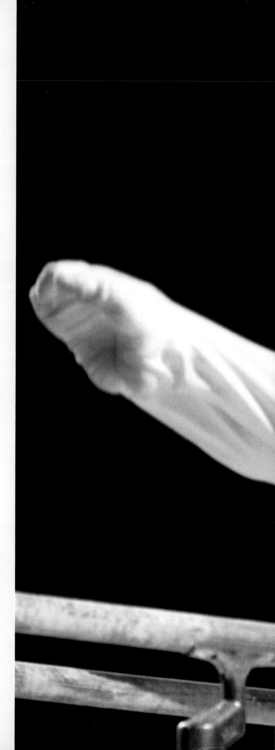

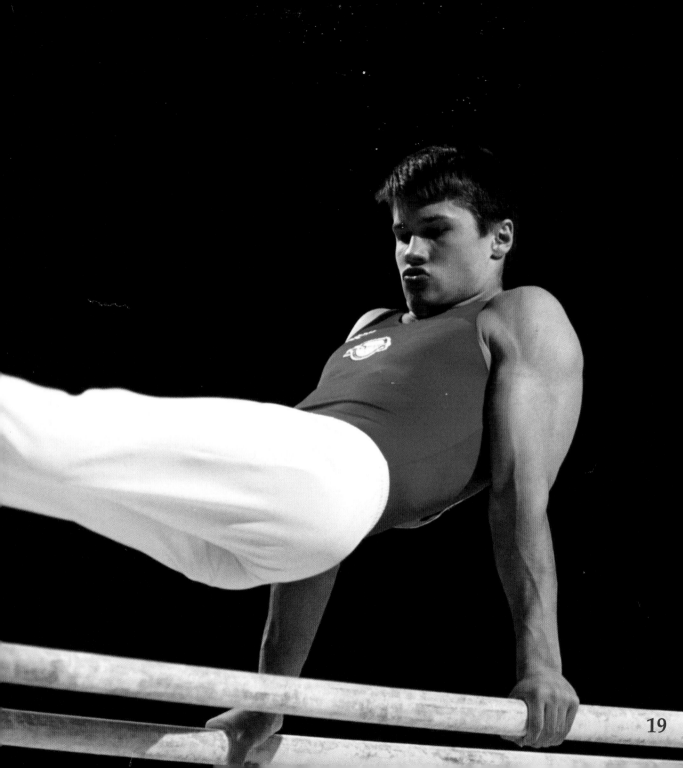

19

Amazing but True!

Friction lets us see meteors. When meteors fall to earth from space, friction is created between the meteors and particles in the air. Heat from friction causes the meteors to glow and burn up. This is why we can see them streak across the night sky.

Hands On: Experiment with Friction

The amount of friction between objects depends on their surfaces and how hard they push against each other. Ask an adult to help you with this activity.

What You Need

shoebox
scissors
1 foot (30.5 centimeters) of string
heavy books
skateboard

What You Do

1. Poke a hole in one end of the shoebox with the scissors. Ask an adult to help you. Tie the string to the shoebox through the hole.
2. Place the shoebox on a carpeted floor. Pull it along with the string.
3. Next, try pulling the shoebox on a wood or other smooth floor.
4. Place some of the books in the shoebox. Pull the box on the wood floor again. Try pulling it on the carpeted floor. Is there a difference?
5. Place the shoebox with the books on the skateboard. Pull it on the wood floor and the carpeted floor. Which was easier to pull?

Did you notice the difference in friction between rough and smooth surfaces? How did the heavy books affect friction? How is rolling friction different from kinetic friction?

Glossary

friction (FRIK-shuhn)—a force produced when two objects rub against each other; friction slows down or stops an object's movement.

kinetic (ki-NET-ik)—having to do with movement, or caused by movement; kinetic friction resists movement from an outside force.

lubricant (LOO-bruh-kuhnt)—a substance, such as oil or grease, that is used to reduce friction between objects

resist (ri-ZIST)—to oppose a force or effect

static (STAT-ik)—having to do with a lack of movement; static friction is the force that causes an object to stay in place without sliding.

Read More

Hunter, Rebecca. *The Facts about Forces and Motion.* Science, the Facts. North Mankato, Minn.: Smart Apple Media, 2005.

Olien, Rebecca. *Motion.* Our Physical World. Mankato, Minn.: Capstone Press, 2005.

Trumbauer, Lisa. *What Is Friction?* Rookie Read-About Science. New York: Children's Press, 2004.

Internet Sites

FactHound offers a safe, fun way to find Internet sites related to this book. All of the sites on FactHound have been researched by our staff.

Here's how:
1. Visit *www.facthound.com*
2. Type in this special code **0736854029** for age-appropriate sites. Or enter a search word related to this book for a more general search.
3. Click on the **Fetch It** button.

FactHound will fetch the best sites for you!

Index